the library of african american arts and culture

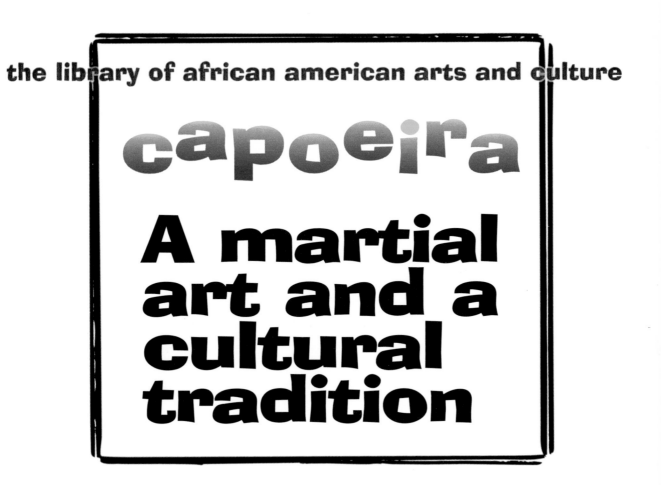

capoeira

A martial art and a cultural tradition

Capoeira is a beautiful martial art with a rich and exciting history.

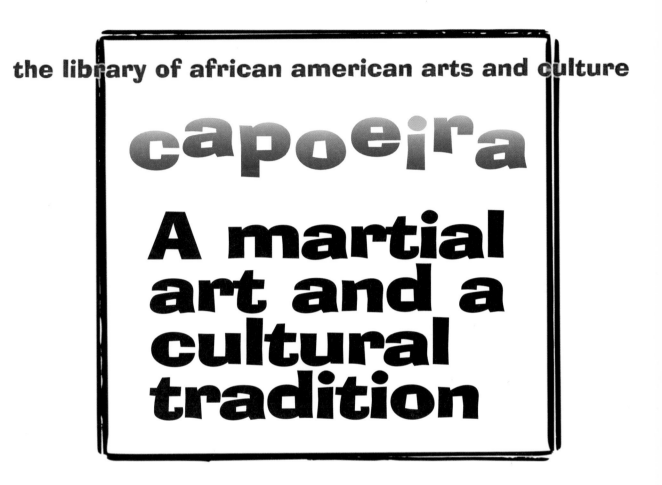

the library of african american arts and culture

capoeira

A martial art and a cultural tradition

jane atwood

rosen publishing group,inc./new york

Published in 1999 by The Rosen Publishing Group, Inc.
29 East 21st Street, New York, NY 10010

Copyright © 1999 by The Rosen Publishing Group, Inc.

First Edition

Library of Congress Cataloging-in-Publication Data

Atwood, Jane.
　　Capoeira: a martial art and a cultural tradition / Jane Atwood.
　　　　p.　cm. — (The library of African American arts and culture)
　　Includes bibliographical references (p.) and index.
　　Summary: Traces the roots and history of the martial art which was developed by Brazilian slaves and combines dance, play, ritual, and self-defense.
　　ISBN 0-8239-1859-9 (lib. bdg.)
　　1. Capoeira (Dance)—Juvenile literature.　[1. Capoeira (Dance)
2. Martial arts.]　I. Title.　II. Series.
GV1796.C145D39　1998
793.3'1--dc21
　　　　　　　　　　　　　　　　　　　　　　　　　　98-42448
　　　　　　　　　　　　　　　　　　　　　　　　　　CIP
　　　　　　　　　　　　　　　　　　　　　　　　　　AC

Manufactured in the United States of America

Capoeira takes place in the center of a circle of musicians, whose music accompanies and influences the game.

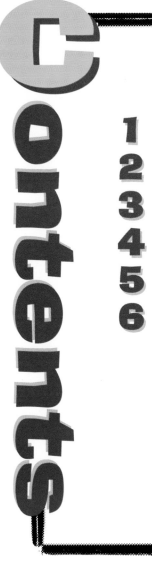

Contents

Introduction

Capoeira (ka-po-AIR-a) is one of the most beautiful and exciting martial arts. African slaves in Brazil developed capoeira hundreds of years ago. It includes elements of fight, play, dance, music, theater, ritual, and philosophy. This combination of elements is very unusual for a martial art; but it is very common in African culture. It is one of the things that makes capoeira so distinctive.

Capoeira is not only a way to defend yourself, it is also a sport that can entertain you. It is said that capoeira put the "art" into "martial art." Capoeira is played to music, and its moves are smooth and graceful. One capoeira master says that the players "move like serpents." In many ways, capoeira resembles dance. But at the same time capoeira is a sport and a game. Capoeira was even one of the arts that inspired break dancing, the African American dance style developed in the 1970s and 1980s.

Capoeira features some spectacular and exciting moves. Some of these are designed to knock a player off his or her feet. Whether a player is standing up or crouched close to the ground, he can have only his hands, feet, and head touching the ground. This rule makes the game even more challenging. For example, imagine doing a cartwheel to kick at your opponent. You have to keep your balance, complete your cartwheel, and defend yourself against your opponent—all at the same time!

Like many of the Asian martial arts, capoeira has a strong philosophy. Players must respect the art, their teachers, each other, and themselves. The great masters of capoeira are honored and admired, even those who died long ago. Their words and wisdom are still passed down to young students today.

This book will explain what capoeira is and how it began. It will describe both the ritual and the game that make up capoeira. And it will tell you about some famous capoeira masters who have helped develop the martial art into its present forms. Finally, at the end of the book, you'll find some places where you can learn capoeira. You, too, can participate in this fun, beautiful, and exciting martial art.

1 what is capoeira?

Take the following: martial arts, jumping, cart-wheeling, dancing, music, chanting, African roots, and Brazilian influence. Roll them into one, and you've got *capoeira*. Capoeira, in its simplest terms, is an expression of movement. But so many different elements make up capoeira that defining it isn't easy.

Capoeira Is a Complex Art

Capoeira is a type of martial art. A martial art is a series of self-defense movements. Martial arts exist in many different lands, such as Africa, China, Japan, Barbados, Brazil, Trinidad, and Tobago. They were invented by warriors hundreds, sometimes thousands, of years ago. For example, African men used dancing as a way to prepare for war. Also,

Capoeira is a complicated art that combines physical strength with artistic expression.

Chinese warriors invented a style of boxing that involved their bare hands and feet. They called it kung fu. You may have seen kung fu in movies and on TV. Jackie Chan, the star of many action/adventure films, practices kung fu. To understand what makes capoeira so special and so different from other martial arts, let's compare it to kung fu.

Like kung fu, capoeira is a series of arm and leg movements. However, in kung fu the two opponents make body contact with each other, often with kicks and hand chops. But a good capoeirista—a person who plays capoeira—is not violent. A capoeirista actually makes very little body contact with her opponent. A player dodges her opponent's moves by bending her knees and moving from side to side. A player does not resist or block her opponent's moves but sways around or under them. While she is moving around, she decides on just the right moment to make her counterstrike. In general, capoeira looks like a dance and has even been called a "martial dance."

Both kung fu and capoeira include takedowns. A takedown is a move that knocks an opponent off his feet. A kung fu player will twist his opponent's arm and flip the opponent over his back. The opponent lands on his back. In capoeira, a player uses spectacular takedowns that incorporate all parts of his body. In one type of takedown, he stands with his back to his oppo-

nent, reaches down between his legs, and grabs his opponent's ankles. The capoeirista then pulls up and knocks the opponent off his feet. However, unlike kung fu, capoeira is acrobatic. It uses moves such as cartwheels.

Another difference between the two martial arts is the use of a standing position. In kung fu and other Asian martial arts, the fighter stands in one position, makes a move, and returns to this position after completing the move. A kung fu fighter doesn't jump around very much. In capoeira, though, a player is constantly on the move. She doesn't stand still. And

Capoeira uses many intricate and spectacular body positions and movements.

11

she doesn't return to any one position after making each move.

According to Bira Almeida, the author of *Capoeira: A Brazilian Art Form*, a capoeirista usually moves around unpredictably. It is very difficult to find a pattern in his actions. Usually there isn't one. Also, a capoeirista uses all the space available to him. He tries to fake out his opponent. A good capoeirista never moves straight toward his opponent, but uses a complicated series of moves that circle around him.

Two Main Types of Capoeira

There are two main types, or styles, of capoeira: Angola and Regional or Regional Senzala.

Capoeira Angola

Capoeira Angola is the original, traditional form of capoeira. Angola is also the hardest form of capoeira to learn. Someone who practices the Angola style is called an Angoleiro.

In the Angola style, the capoeiristas play to slow music and perform movements deliberately and carefully. Often the game begins to very slow music, but the music speeds up as the game progresses. The moves in Angola are closer to the ground and not as acrobatic as in other forms.

Angola places great importance on malícia, which is

the art of being tricky. A player should never show strengths or weaknesses. He should be able to fool his opponent and to take him by surprise.

Capoeira Regional and Regional Senzala

Capoeira Regional is based on a set of moves developed by the great Mestre (Master) Bimba in the 1930s. Mestre Bimba put certain moves together so that students would be able to learn them more easily.

Capoeira Regional places great importance on fancy kicks and takedowns. The movements that are closer to the ground (and important in the Angola style) are not as crucial in Regional. This is because Mestre Bimba considered them less effective for self-defense. He also changed some of the kicks from the Angola style to make them more aggressive. Since the moves are aggressive and quick in Regional, the rhythm of the music is also fast. It doesn't start slowly, as it does in capoeira Angola.

Critics of capoeira Regional say it lacks the improvisation (ability to make things up as you go along), unpredictability, and individuality of capoeira Angola. However, despite these criticisms, capoeira Regional has become very popular. Today most capoeira academies, or schools, in Brazil teach some form of capoeira Regional.

Capoeira Regional Senzala was developed by a group of Regional capoeiristas in the 1960s. They created new ways of teaching capoeira and further changed Mestre Bimba's movements. Capoeira Regional and Regional Senzala are so closely associated with each other that the two words are often used interchangeably.

The Batizado

Capoeira, no matter what the style, can be difficult to learn. It takes years of practice. Once a student becomes skilled, he is initiated into the world of capoeira in a batizado, or baptism. A student can be baptized only when his mestre is confident of his commitment to capoeira. Not only must a student show his superior skill, but he must show his dedication and discipline. This usually happens after two months of practice. At the baptism, the student is given a nickname by which he is known to other capoeiristas. During baptisms, students also have a chance to play and test their skills against more experienced players.

Why Is It Called Capoeira?

Scholars have many different ideas about how capoeira got its name. However, no one can be entirely certain. Antenor Nascentes, a great Brazilian researcher of word origins, said the capoeira game or fight is similar to a bird called a capoeira. The male

capoeira
has fierce
fights with other
male birds who go near
his female mate. He says the skill
of the male capoeira birds resembles that of capoeira players.

Some Brazilian writers
claim the word *capoeira*
is from the Tupi Indian
language. Others trace it
to the Indian (not Native
American) language of
Guarani, the root of most
Brazilian Indian dialects. Other
people claim it comes from

Capoeira requires skill, agility, and
concentration.

Portuguese, the major language in Brazil. In
Portuguese, *capoeira* means a "big chicken coop" or a
"place where birds are flattened." It can also mean a
"basket made with sticks for caging roosters and chick-
ens" or a "chicken thief."

One African scholar believes the word *capoeira* is
from the Kikongo word *kipura/kipula*. Both *pura* and
pula mean "to flutter" or "to flit from place to place."
The terms describe roosters' back-and-forth, up-and-
down, and turning-around movements in a fight.
Kipura, in the Kongo culture, is someone who bases
his fighting style on that of roosters. Also, the

15

Portuguese word *capao* means "rooster." Capoeira has often been compared to a rooster fight.

As you can see, there are many different ideas about where the word *capoeira* came from. However, no matter where it got its name, capoeira is becoming more familiar to people around the world. More students than ever before are learning about and practicing this martial art.

2 the history of capoeira

Although some people consider capoeira an African martial art, capoeira did not begin in Africa. But its origins and influences were mainly African. African slaves living in Brazil created capoeira. It was a way for them to fight enemies and defend themselves. By doing capoeira together, Africans far from their homeland also could share a common experience and honor their own legacy.

An African Influence

Before they came to Brazil, African peoples practiced several types of martial arts. These martial arts had a huge influence on the development of capoeira in Brazil.

For example, many people in Angola and Kongo studied martial arts. One of the most popular martial arts was sanga. Sanga is an ancient war dance created as early as 1594. Dictionaries of

African slaves living in Brazil are usually credited with the development of capoeira.

Where Is Kongo?

When Kongo is spelled with a K, it refers to the Bakongo people and their ancient kingdom in central Africa. The Bakongo, which means the Kongo people, live mainly in the modern countries of Angola, Congo, and Zaire. Their total population is about five million. The Bakongo have strong ties to the powerful Kingdom of Kongo. The Kingdom of Kongo began to form around AD 1200 and ended in the late 1600s, when the Portuguese defeated it.

When Congo is spelled with a C, it refers to the current political states. These states are along the Western coast of Central Africa. In 1960, they formed the Democratic Republic of Congo, which is known as Zaire today.

the Kongo language define sanga as a sword dance. The word can also mean "to triumph," "to leap with joy," or "to intermingle."

Warfare in Angola and the Kongo often involved hand-to-hand combat using short swords and axes. To defend themselves, warriors had to use many evasive movements—moves made to avoid something. Dance and evasive movements are also important in capoeira.

John Thornton, a scholar of African history, points out, "Military dancing was a major part of the African war culture. African cultures used dancing as a way to prepare for war. It helped to train warriors to move quickly and gracefully during hand-to-hand combat." Many of the skills crucial to military dancing are important in capoeira, too.

Scholars cannot agree upon which dance or martial art capoeira Angola is based. The great capoeirista Vicente Pastinha said his teacher told him it came from the n'golo dance. *N'golo* means "dance of the zebras." This dance was performed by young males in Angola during the celebration of young girls' puberty. The best dancer could choose a young girl to be his wife without paying a dowry, or marriage fee, to the bride's family. Other experts argue capoeira isn't based on a single dance or martial art, but mixes together elements of several dances and martial arts.

Africans Arrive in Brazil

As you learned earlier, African slaves in Brazil began capoeira. The slaves were owned by Portuguese people living in Brazil. In 1500, the Portuguese landed in the area that would later become Brazil. Their fleet of thirteen ships was bound for India, where they traded goods such as black powder, fabric, and brandy. Storms over the Atlantic Ocean set them off course. The Portuguese arrived in Brazil by accident. However, many of them decided to stay there. The Tupi Indian tribe helped them adjust to life in Brazil. The Tupi taught them how to adapt to this lush new land.

The Portuguese started huge farms, called plantations, of cotton, tobacco, coffee, and sugarcane in Brazil. But they needed many workers to help the plantations run properly. They forced Indian tribes to work as slaves on the plantations, but many Indians became sick and died, or they escaped.

The Portuguese decided to get slaves from Africa to replace the Indians. They forced hundreds of Africans aboard ships bound for Brazil. In all, about two million Africans were brought to Brazil. Many of the Africans were from Angola. They had to leave their material possessions behind, but they carried their language, stories, and traditions with them.

Capoeira Is Born

In Brazil, some African slaves managed to escape. They banded together to fight against Portuguese soldiers and to free other slaves. The most famous group of African fighters was called the Quilombo dos Palmares, founded in 1595. They named their group Palmares because there were many palm trees in the area. Some experts claim capoeira was born in this community. However, no written records from that time exist. We do know capoeira was begun by African slaves in Brazil, not by people in Africa.

The African slaves' owners forbade them to practice capoeira. The Portuguese were afraid that their slaves would become skilled fighters and would rise up against them. Any slave caught doing capoeira could be put to death. As a result, capoeira was taught in secret in the senzalas, or slave quarters, and passed down from generation to generation.

Capoeiristas on the Run

In 1822, the Portuguese living in Brazil declared their independence from Portugal, and the nation of Brazil was born. Later, in 1888, the Brazilian government ended slavery. Many of the freed Africans stayed in the country. However, the Brazilian government still discouraged capoeira.

The government officially outlawed capoeira in 1892, but many capoeiristas avoided arrest. One way they did this was by using nicknames. It was common for capoeiristas to have two or three nicknames. The police would only know them by their nicknames instead of by their real names. This made it very difficult for the police to find the capoeiristas or discover their true identities. Even today, a capoeirista is given a nickname during his baptism.

After the African Brazilian slaves were freed, many could not find work and fell upon hard times. The Brazilians of Portuguese descent often did not want to hire them because they were considered lower class. Capoeira also had a bad reputation, since many people associated it with the poor.

Some of the African Brazilians turned to crime to earn a living because of these hard times. Most capoeiristas worked together in groups called maltas or braboas. Maltas had from twenty to one hundred capoeiristas as members. When someone wanted to join a malta, he had to go through a secret initiation, or ceremony.

Politicians and business owners hired the maltas to threaten, rob, or beat up their opponents and competitors. The maltas would rob tavern keepers for cash and beat up police patrols. But they never used guns in fights. Capoeiristas were proud they didn't need guns to win a fight. They could win using their capoeira skills alone. Maltas increased capoeira's poor reputation, and the martial art became associated with crime and criminals.

One capoeirista who became an underground hero was Manoel Henrique. His nickname was Mestre Besouro. Mestre Besouro was famous for his battles with police and his daring escapes from death. *Besouro* means "beetle" in Portuguese. Like a beetle, Mestre Besouro could "fly away" just when he

seemed hopelessly trapped. He believed he was protected from bullets and knives by magic. According to
legend, Mestre Besouro was killed by a knife that had
a spell put upon it to counteract, or act against, his
magic. Many of the most famous chants sung during
capoeira games are about Mestre Besouro.

A Growing Popularity

In 1920, capoeira became legal in Brazil. Mestre
Bimba, a capoeira master, opened the first capoeira
academy in Brazil in 1932. During the 1930s,
capoeiristas could practice only in areas that were reg-
istered with the police.

Later, during the 1960s, a new style of capoeira
developed, called Regional Senzala. Some capoeira
masters wanted to make the sport easier to learn or to
emphasize different elements.

Capoeira Regional was invented in the 1930s by the
great Mestre Bimba, but it didn't become popular until
the 1960s. Capoeira Regional uses a great deal of
organized training and kicking, whereas capoeira
Angola does not use fixed series of movements.
Regional Senzala is similar to Regional and was developed by a group of Regional capoeiristas. From that
time on, the traditional style of capoeira became
known as capoeira Angola.

During the 1970s, capoeira began to move beyond
the borders of Brazil. Former students of great mestres

moved out of the country and began teaching others around the world.

In 1972, the Brazilian government recognized capoeira as an official sport. Capoeiristas could compete in local and national competitions. The Brazilian Boxing Federation governed the competitions. But not everything went smoothly. The members of the federation could not agree on whether capoeira Angola or Regional Senzala should be played. They also argued about the scoring and about what to name certain moves. Some mestres even refused to compete in competitions because they did not agree with the federation's rules.

Although capoeira's reputation had improved over the years, the sport still had problems. Many people were unhappy that Regional Senzala had become more popular than the traditional capoeira Angola. In a newspaper article, one capoeirista said tourists threatened to turn the "ritual into a show" because, as it became more well known, capoeira was moving away from its traditions. He also said modern Regional Senzala teachers had turned a "game and art into a sport with rules and regulations." This capoeirista felt many of the interesting and unique elements of capoeira were being lost.

Looking Toward the Future

Even today capoeira continues to grow and change. It

is still very popular in Brazil, which has the second-largest African population in the world. However, people all over the world are now doing capoeira. Also, capoeira Angola has become popular again. More people began to practice the Angola style during the mid-1980s. Now many capoeiristas teach a blend of both styles. Finally, the International Olympic Committee has recognized capoeira. Capoeiristas will demonstrate the sport in the 2004 Olympic Games.

Brazilian capoeiristas are some of the best in the world.

3 a sacred ritual

Ritual is an important part of capoeira. A ritual is a ceremony or sacred event. A capoeira ritual can include music and chanting, which accompany the players' movements.

Capoeira begins when people form a circle around two players. The circle, or roda, is made up of the musicians and spectators (people who watch the game). At the top of the circle is the bateria, an ensemble of musicians and singers. The musicians play several different instruments. Three of these, the berimbau, the atabaque, and the pandeiro, are required for a capoeira game. Often, the musicians play two other instruments: the reco-reco and the agogô.

The Most Important Instrument

The most important instrument in capoeira is the berimbau. It is said this instrument originally came

Instrument used in the capoeira roda

from Tunga, Africa. The berimbau is a musical bow; it is made out of wood bent with a steel string. The wooden part is called a vara or a verga and is about fifty-six inches long. The steel string is called an arame. The bow is held in the musician's left hand along with a coin or stone to change the vibration of the steel string. Plucking the string makes a buzzing sound.

Attached near one of the bow's ends is a cabaça, a hollowed-out gourd that makes the sound resonate, or loudly repeat. When a thin, flexible stick, called a baqueta or a vaqueta, strikes the bowstring, it produces sound. This sound is more rhythmic than the buzzing made by the coin or stone. The baqueta and a caxixí are held together in the right hand. The caxixí is made out of woven straw and has dried beans or pebbles in it. The caxixí, with its rattle, makes the berimbau sound richer.

Berimbaus are made with tender loving care. One mestre says the wood used for a berimbau must be cut from a live tree on just the right day and under a "proper moon." After the wood is dried and sanded, it must be warmed over a fire and soaked in linseed oil.

Different styles of capoeira may use slightly different rodas. An Angola roda uses three kinds of berimbaus: the gunga, or bass; the berimbau médio, or mid-tone; and the viola, or high tone. Together, the three berimbaus have an amazing sound. Their sound decides the pace of the game. Is the game fast and violent, or slow and mischievous? When the game becomes too intense,

**There are certain rhythms that
most berimbau musicians know.
Here are some of them:**

São Bento Grande: A light (casual) game

São Bento Pequeno: Samba of Capoeira

Banquela: The Knife Game

Santa Maria: The Measured Game

Ave Maria: The Capoeira Hymn

Amazonas: The Middle Game

Lúna: The Creeping Game

**Cavalaria: A signal announcing approaching
strangers**

the music can also calm the players. Some call the berimbau "the soul of capoeira."

In other rodas, only one berimbau is played. The berimbau player is usually the mestre, who is also in charge of the game. The mestre pairs players to play against each other and begins and ends games.

Years ago, when capoeira was outlawed, some berimbau rhythms were played to warn people of a police raid. When the capoeiristas heard that beat, they scattered in all directions.

Other Instruments

The atabaque is the second necessary instrument. The atabaque is a drum that a musician plays with his hands. It's similar to a conga drum.

The third instrument is the pandeiro, or tambourine. Often a roda will have at least two pandeiros. In Mestre Bimba's school, the pandeiro was made out of skin from a boa constrictor!

In addition to the berimbau, the atabaque, and the pandeiro, the reco-reco and the agogô may also be used in the roda. A reco-reco is an eighteen-inch-long section of bamboo or gourd cut with notches. A musician plays it by scraping it with a thin stick. The reco-reco is becoming rare in rodas today. The agogô is a cowbell struck with a stick or thin metal rod.

The ritual of capoeira begins when two players enter the roda and kneel at the foot of the berimbau. The mestre or the first player sings a ladainha, a ritual song sung before the beginning of the game. Ladainhas are sung in Angola

(From the top, counterclockwise) Capoeira instruments include the atabaque, the pandeiro, the agogô, and the reco-reco.

Here are several verses of a traditional capoeira song. It talks about an important idea—that material possessions won't last forever because you can't take them with you when you die.

No Céu entra quem merece,
No Terra vale é quem tem.
Passar bem ou passar mal,
Tudo na vida é passar, camará.

You enter heaven on your merits;
Here on Earth what you own is all that counts.
Fare you well or fare you poorly,
All on this Earth is but farewell, comrade.

games. Regional capoeiristas do not use them. The mestre uses a ladainha to praise or tease the two players. The ladainha is answered by a chorus sung by the people in the circle. After the chorus is finished, the opponent can also answer with a song of his own. If he doesn't, the first player begins another song called a corrido. The corrido signals the players to begin movements. A musician will take over the corrido as the jogo de capoeira, or game of capoeira, begins.

Chants

A chula is the chant or song that follows the ladainha. Chulas often talk about religion, important ideas, or philosophical views about the world. Capoeira students must learn these songs in Portuguese. However, most of the songs do not use proper Portuguese. They often

This capoeira song was written by the great Mestre Pastinha. It talks about one of his religious beliefs.

Ie Maior é deus
Ie, maior é deus
Pequeno sou eu
O que sei, o que tenho
Foi deus quem me deu
Mas na roda da capoeira
Grande pequeno sou eu

God is greater than I am
God is great; I am small
Everything that I have
Everything that I know comes from God
But, although I am small before God
In the Roda of Capoeira
I discover my own greatness

contain words of African origin. Mestres have written many of today's chants, but some are of unknown origin. Many of these are believed to have been sung by the early African slaves in Brazil.

Other songs are used to taunt the players. In one song, the singer says, "Moleque e tu," or "You are a bum." Here's another song that teases the players.

Dá, dá, dá no nego
No nego você não dá
Dá, dá, dá no nego
esse nego é danado,

    Go beat that guy
    I bet you can't get him
    Go beat that guy
    That guy is something else

Esse nego é o cão
Dá, dá, dá no nego
Esse nego te agarra
Te joga no chão
Dá, dá, dá no nego

    He is very tough
    Go beat that guy
    That guy will grab you and
    Throw you on the ground
    Go beat that guy

4 playing the game

Although it is a ritual, capoeira is also a game. In some ways, it is similar to other games and sports, such as basketball, baseball, and soccer. Capoeira has rules that players must follow. Also, it often has uniforms capoeiristas must wear. If you want to do capoeira, first you must learn about the game and how it is played.

The Capoeira Circle

As the musicians play their berimbaus, two players crouch at the foot of these instruments. They pay their respects to the game. During the chants, the two players touch the ground and trace imaginary signs that signify the closing of their bodies and strengthening of their spirits. A body that is open is considered defenseless. A closed body is spiritually protected. This ritual is

The capoeira circle, or roda

called a mandinga. Years ago, a capoeirista would bless himself three times before the game started. Modern capoeiristas don't usually do this anymore.

The players follow the rhythm of the music and chants. The first player sings the corrido. Afterward, the players lift their bodies into a position that looks like a handstand; their heads don't touch the ground. Their upper bodies are balanced on their bent arms while their legs are raised into the air. The players then return to their crouched position, and play begins.

The musicians in the capoeira roda are very important. Their music is not only part of the ritual, it also determines the way the players play the game.

The Game Begins

The players move to the center of the roda with only their hands and feet touching the ground. The object of the game is for a player to get her opponent into a position in which she can't defend herself. Then the player hits—but doesn't actually touch—her opponent with a blow, kick, or sweep to knock the opponent off her feet and onto her back. (In general, capoeiristas do not touch their opponents. Pretending to strike an opponent is considered more impressive than actually hitting her.) The opponent then loses the game because only her head, hands, or feet can touch the ground.

A Sample Capoeira Game

Here's how a typical game might be played.

One of the players makes the first move, a kick. His opponent dodges the kick by bending his knees and swaying under the player's leg. By doing so, his opponent is able to avoid the kick.

The opponent responds by springing onto his hands and kicking out his right foot. The first player bends down at the waist, dodging the kick. He raises his arms to signify a passo a dois, a move in which both players take three steps forward and three steps backward while touching each other's hands. Then he moves for

The Cordão

A Regional capoeirista wears a cordão, a thick string tied around the waist, to indicate his or her level of skill. The colors of the cordão come from the Brazilian flag: green, yellow, blue, and white. Capoeira Angola academies don't use cordãos.

Capoeiristas' ranks are mestre (Master) and contra mestre (assistant instructor). However, Mestre Bimba had his own system, or rank. The accepted order of rank in capoeira includes:

- the calouro (freshman) wears no uniform and no cordão
- the batisado (baptized) wears, as he or she progresses in skill:

  a white uniform and no cordão

  a white uniform and green cordão for moves of all styles

  a white uniform and yellow cordão for floor and takedown moves

  a white uniform and blue cordão for jumping and acrobatic moves
- the formado (graduated) wears a cordão braided with green, yellow, and blue
- the especializado (specialized) wears a special emblem for attending special workshops
- the mestre wears a white cordão

a takedown (a move intended to knock an opponent down) of his opponent.

The player drops to the ground, balancing on his hands, and wraps his lower legs around his opponent's ankle. But the opponent is too fast. He does a cartwheel and frees his ankles. After doing more movements, either player can end the game by spinning and then shaking his opponent's hand. If neither player is taken down by his opponent, the player who showed the most skill wins the game. Generally, a game takes about two minutes, and long games can last for up to fifteen minutes. Capoeira classes begin and end with a salute and the cry of "*Salve!*" which means "Freedom!"

Some Rules to Remember

As you learned earlier, capoeiristas usually do not touch their opponents. A pretend strike is more impressive than an actual hit. During some moves, players seem to be moving in slow motion. A skilled player will creatively weave his or her strikes, kicks, and evasions during the game. There is no set order to the movements; they are improvised, or made up as the game happens. Since players make up their own moves, the game is always exciting and unique.

Also, players use very few offensive movements. An offensive movement is one that attacks your opponent. A defensive movement is one that protects you from an attack by your opponent. Capoeiristas usually don't

The girl makes an offensive move; the boy uses a defensive one.

block moves; they simply move along with them. A player is supposed to act cowardly when his opponent strikes, and then display his own skill during his next move. Pretending to act cowardly before launching an impressive counterstrike shows the player is being tricky.

Capoeiristas use very few hand movements. Although some open-handed strikes are permitted, hits with closed fists are forbidden. Some scholars believe this practice can be traced back to the slaves, who practiced capoeira while their hands were bound in chains. They weren't able to use their hands very well because of the chains.

Other experts argue an ancient African tradition explains the small number of hand movements. The tradition says hands should be used for good work, such as creating things, and feet should be used for bad work, such as punishing and destroying things. One proverb

What to Wear?

Today students of capoeira don't wear shoes during class, and men sometimes don't wear shirts. However, capoeiristas of years ago did. No proper Brazilian went out in public without shoes or a shirt. To do so showed that one was poor. Capoeiristas frequently showed up to a roda in their fanciest clothes!

says, "*Mooko my tunga, malu mu diatikisa*," which means "Hands are to build, feet are to destroy." Whatever the reason, foot and leg movements are more important than hand movements in capoeira. Finally, traditional Angola players frown upon too much bodily contact.

Key Elements

There are six important features in capoeira: malícia,

complementation, beautiful movement, slow rhythm, the importance of ritual, and theatrical aspects. The most skilled capoeiristas can display all these elements in their games.

Malícia

Malícia is the art of being tricky or deceptive. A skilled player must anticipate her opponent's moves and start her own counterattack before her opponent is finished attacking. She will also try to look vulnerable until her opponent attacks. When the attack comes, however, she is ready to fight.

In other words, malícia is being aware and ready. A player must never lose sight of her opponent. Some players never look directly at their opponent. They use their peripheral (side) vision to watch them. Doing so tricks their opponents into thinking they aren't paying attention.

Malícia is important in the Angola style, but it is not stressed in capoeira Regional. Often mestres warn their students not to use too much malícia. A popular Brazilian saying is, *"Malandro demais se atrapalha,"* which says that when one tries to be too tricky, he only confuses himself.

Complementation

When playing capoeira, your moves should complement,

Capoeiristas do defensive moves, such as the quedo de quatro shown here, to avoid strikes rather than block them.

or add to, your opponent's. All the moves should flow together. In this way, capoeira is similar to a cutting session in jazz or a jam session in rock. In these sessions, the musicians try to outplay each other. Everyone's efforts add up to create a great piece of music. In a capoeira game, both players' moves should combine to make something beautiful, creative, and unique.

Beautiful Movement

It is not enough for a capoeirista to beat his opponent. He must prove his skill by winning with style. His movements have to be effective, but they also have to be beautiful. Movements shouldn't be choppy or robotic. They should flow gracefully and beautifully. Many people say that capoeira resembles a dance because of its beautiful movements.

Slow Rhythm

The movements in capoeira Angola are generally slow and deliberate. In capoeira, as in some other martial arts, many people assume if you can perform a movement slowly and perfectly, you can also do it quickly and effectively. The slow rhythm in capoeira

Capoeira is extremely beautiful; at times, it looks like a dance.

41

enhances the beautiful and skillful appearance of the movements.

Importance of Ritual

Capoeira Angola is complicated and has a very complex ritual. It has many rules. If someone does not know all of these unwritten rules, other capoeiristas consider him an inferior player. The mandinga, which you learned about earlier, is the tracing of an imaginary sign on the ground before play begins. This ritual is very short and might not seem important. However, a skilled capoeirista will know and respect every part of capoeira rituals.

Theatrical Aspects

When capoeiristas are playing, they are also entertaining an audience of spectators, just as if they were in a theater. A capoeirista plays the jogo, or game, not only with her opponent, but also with the audience in the roda. The game's acrobatic movements and the players' skills should please and amuse the spectators.

5 mastering the movements

Capoeira is made up of some basic movements. These movements differ slightly between the Angola and Regional styles. A beginner must master these simpler moves before he or she can learn breathtaking kicks and takedowns. To be a truly skilled capoeirista, one must master the most basic moves and then build upon them.

There are three basic movements in capoeira, in addition to the kicks, defensive movements, and takedowns. These movements are called the ginga, the negativa and the rolê, and the aú.

A player practicing the ginga

The Ginga

Ginga (ZHIN-ga) means "to swing." It comes from the Portuguese word *gingar*, which means "to sway from side to side while walking," or "to waddle." Ginga is a set of movements done standing up. A skilled capoeirista will constantly move around to dodge her opponent and to prepare her own moves. A player will stand facing her opponent and stretch her left foot backward. She brings her feet together about shoulders' width apart. Then she moves her right foot back, and then the left back again. Now she moves forward or side to side.

Within the ginga, there are three parts. The passada is the movement of the feet, the balanço is the swaying or swinging of the body with the feet firmly planted, and the jogo de corpo is the movement of the upper body. Angola mestres let students make up their own ginga. Regional mestres are strict about ginga positions. In capoeira Regional, the ginga is a structured set of movements.

The Negativa and the Rolê

The negativa (neg-a-CHEE-va) and the rolê (ho-LEH) are the basic capoeira movements performed on the floor. Angola negativas are close to the ground. In an Angola negativa, a player is outstretched with his upper body twisted to one side and both palms on the ground. Remember, only his hands and feet can touch the floor, or he will be disqualified. In a Regional negativa, a player is in the same position, except that his upper body is upright, and he has only one hand on the floor.

A rolê is a transitional move, which means it is used to switch from one move to another. Players use a rolê to move from the negativa to the ginga. Basically, the rolê is a way to stand up. While a player is balanced on the floor in a negativa, he twists his upper body, which forces him to flip his bent leg over his outstretched leg and bring himself to a standing position.

The Aú

The aú (ah-OO) is a cartwheel. Cartwheels can be used as offensive or defensive moves. In the Angola style, the capoeirista's knees are bent. A Regional aú is done with straight legs. An experienced capoeirista may defend herself against an offensive aú by giving her opponent a head butt while the opponent is in the middle of her cartwheel. Or she may drop to the floor, while kicking out her leg to hit her opponent's hand. This move will knock her opponent off balance, and her opponent will fall to the floor.

The aú is one of capoeira's most exciting and acrobatic movements.

Kicks

A capoeirista can use several types of kicks to attack an opponent.

• The armada involves spinning and kicking. With your back to your opponent, you twist your upper body around until you can see the other player. As you continue to spin around, you kick outward.

• A martelo-do-chão is done from a negativa. From the negativa, you flip to the side, supported by both hands. During the turn, you kick out the bent leg.

• A martelo-em-pé resembles a karate kick. Standing with your side to your opponent, you raise the leg closest to your opponent. You bend your leg at the knee and then kick out. Swiftly kick outward, extending your leg and aiming the top of your foot at your opponent.

• A meia lua de compasso is the

(From the top, clockwise) An armada, a martelo-em-pé, and a meia lua de compasso "kick of kicks." You begin standing up and then bend at the waist, placing both hands on the floor. You continue to look at your opponent through your legs. In this move, the placement of your hands on the floor is important. Your left hand is placed higher on the floor than your right hand. Your right leg is then kicked out and up. While your right leg is still in the air, you spin clockwise. As you are spinning around, you gradually stand up, placing your right leg behind you.

Defensive Movements

Capoeiristas do defensive movements to avoid kicks, not to block them. There are four basic defensive movements.

• The cocorinha dodges a blow by dropping and crouching to the ground. One hand protects your head, and the other touches the floor.

The cocorinha, shown here, is one of capoeira's four basic defensive movements.

• The resistência is like the cocorinha, except that one of your legs is outstretched.
• The queda de quatro looks similar to the way a crab walks. Your hands and feet are on the ground, and the front of your body faces the sky.
• The esquiva avoids a blow when you are standing with your feet apart and with one of your legs behind your body. You lunge forward and place one hand on the ground.

Takedowns

After a capoeirista has learned ginga, kicks, and defensive movements, he is ready to learn takedowns. Takedowns are difficult to do and are perfected only after lots of practice. A capoeirista performs a takedown when he is attacked by his opponent. He must do it quickly for it to be effective.

• The rasteira is one of capoeira's most well known movements. In a rasteira, you drop to your side with only your feet and hands touching the floor. One leg is bent, and one arm is stretched over your head. Your straight leg is swung out at the opponent. When you do this, the opponent should fall onto his back. (He has lost the game because only his feet, hands, and head can touch the ground.) You con-

48   Takedowns, such as the cruz, shown here, are some of the hardest moves for a capoeirista to learn.

tinue swinging your leg around and bring your body upright.

• An arrastão is often used when an opponent is launching a punch. You dodge the punch by bending down at the waist and grabbing your opponent's legs. You do this by placing your hands behind your opponent's knees. With great strength and quickness, you pull your opponent's legs out from under her.

• A boca de calça is basically the same as an arrastão, except you grab only one of your opponent's legs. In the boca de calça de costas, you stand with your back to your opponent. You jump backward, reach down, and grab your opponent's ankles. You pull his ankles forward and up, knocking the opponent onto his back.

• A cruz is done when an opponent is kicking. You bend under the kick so that your opponent's leg is on your back. You then straighten your body, knocking your opponent off balance.

• A tesoura is a takedown that seems to defy gravity. You jump up and lock your legs around your opponent's legs. You then place your hands on the ground for balance and, with your legs, pull your opponent's legs out from under her.

6 masters past and present

Throughout the history of capoeira, mestres have been changing and developing the sport. Their many contributions have made capoeira into the martial art it is today. Mestres from long ago are often legendary, and modern masters are still teaching students and influencing capoeira.

Three Hits: Mestre Bimba

Mestre Bimba's real name was Manoel dos Reis Machado. He died in 1974, but remains legendary for opening the first capoeira academy and for inventing capoeira Regional.

Bimba was born in 1900 in the city of Salvador, where capoeira was played on the waterfront. His father taught him batuque, an African martial dance similar to capoeira. When Bimba was twelve, he began learning capoeira from Bentinho, an African from Angola.

Bimba became known as a fierce fighter. His nick-name was "Três Pancadas," or "Three Hits," because it was said his opponents could take no more than three of his hits. In 1936, he challenged all capoeiris-tas to fight him. Three people accepted. He easily defeated all three. No match lasted longer than seventy seconds.

Bimba opened the first capoeira academy in 1932. He named his school Centro de Cultura Física e Capoeira Regional. Bimba liked the fighting aspects of capoeira. In his own academy he could teach capoeira the way he wanted—emphasizing the fighting qualities and downplaying the African cultural aspects.

Bimba's new style of capoeira was called capoeira Regional. He incorporated sweeping movements from batuque. He also created a new way of teaching capoeira by developing sequences, or series, of moves. The sequences allowed students to learn capoeira Regional more quickly than capoeira Angola. But Bimba was a tough teacher. Few students achieved the rank of mestre. Mestre Bimba gave out only ten master diplomas to students in his life.

Bimba encouraged middle- and upper-class Brazilians, such as high school and college students, to take lessons. He wanted to improve capoeira's image.

Today many people agree Bimba turned capoeira from a poor man's sport into a respected one.

The Philosopher of Capoeira: Mestre Pastinha

Mestre Pastinha, whose real name was Vicente Ferreira Pastinha, was another legendary capoeirista. Pastinha was born in 1889 to a Spanish father and an African mother. When he was ten years old, he was the frequent victim of a bully. An African from Angola named Benedito once saw him and the bully fighting. Afterward Benedito told the boy he could teach him capoeira Angola to defend himself. Pastinha was a quick learner and became a brilliant capoeirista.

Pastinha opened his own capoeira academy several years after Bimba did. Whereas Bimba was the great inventor, Pastinha was the great traditionalist. Pastinha taught only capoeira Angola at his school. He wanted his students to understand the practice, philosophy, and traditions of pure capoeira.

In 1964, Pastinha wrote the first book on capoeira, entitled *Capoeira Angola*. He also wrote many poetic capoeira songs. He became known as the "Philosopher of Capoeira." Two years later, the Brazilian government asked Pastinha to go to Senegal in western Africa to demonstrate capoeira at the First International Festival of Black Arts.

Pastinha's academy became very well known. But the government decided to rebuild the area around his school. They took over the building, but promised Pastinha they would return it to him. Sadly, he never got his building back or reopened his academy. He died in 1981.

After his death, Mestre Pastinha received a great honor. In a brochure celebrating what would have been the Mestre's 100th birthday, the Brazilian state of Bahia declared him part of the Heritage of Bahia.

53

A Modern Master: Mestre João Grande

Mestre João Grande, or João Olivera dos Santos, is one of the greatest capoeiristas alive today. As a young boy in the late 1930s, João liked to learn about nature. He intently studied the strike of a snake and the flight of a bird. This interest in nature would affect the way he played capoeira in the years to come.

Because he had to work on his family's farm, João didn't begin to learn capoeira until he was twenty years old. But João learned capoeira very quickly and became one of Mestre Pastinha's top students. Pastinha gave him the nickname Gavião, which means hawk. Pastinha called João a hawk because of the way he swept down on his opponent.

João Grande, as he was called, quickly became one of the most respected capoeiristas in the

Brazilian state of Bahia. Very few opponents would play him in street rodas. They knew of his great skill and didn't want to lose against him. João was so well known that when Carybe, a painter famous for his work on African culture in Bahia, wanted to paint capoeira, he chose João as his model.

In 1968, Pastinha awarded João his diploma of capoeira. He was then known as Mestre João Grande and began teaching at Pastinha's academy. After Pastinha died in 1981, João dropped out of the capoeira world for a few years. However, two of his former students finally convinced him to return to teaching capoeira.

João Grande's reputation continued to grow. In 1989, he toured the United States to demonstrate capoeira Angola. When he returned to Brazil, the government awarded him the Brazilian National Sports Medal of Merit. The following year he again traveled to the United States to present capoeira at the National Black Arts Festival in Atlanta, Georgia, and to the mayor of New York City. João Grande then moved to New York City and opened an academy there. He still lives and teaches in New York City and has the only full-time capoeira academy in the United States.

Capoeira is many different things. It is a dance, a sport, a martial art, and a way of life. It also teaches many different lessons. Capoeira trains you to battle difficult experiences while staying flexible and open. It prepares you to respond to social violence with evasion and grace. It helps build physical and spiritual strength. Finally, capoeira teaches you to use wisdom to create a balanced and productive life.

Capoeira is much more than simply a martial art. It can teach you things such as strength of character, discipline, and wisdom.

agogô Cowbell that is struck with a stick or thin metal rod.

aú Cartwheel.

berimbau Musical bow; most important instrument in capoeira.

capoeira Martial art developed by Africans in Brazil that includes elements of fight, play, dance, music, theater, ritual, and philosophy.

capoeira Angola Traditional style of capoeira.

capoeira Regional Modern style of capoeira developed by Mestre Bimba.

defensive movement Move that protects you from an attack by your opponent.

ginga Basic side and back movements.

improvise To create or make up something as it happens.

malícia Art of being tricky or cunning; savvy.

malta Band of thieves who practiced capoeira.

martial art Series of self-defense movements.

negativa Basic movement performed on the floor.

offensive movement Move that attacks your opponent.

opponent Someone whom you play against and try to beat in a game.

philosophy Group of beliefs.

reco-reco Musical instrument that is a long section of bamboo or gourd cut with notches; played by scraping with a thin stick.

ritual Ceremony or sacred event.

roda Circle formed for playing capoeira.

rolê Basic movement performed on the floor.

spectator Someone who watches an event.

takedown Move that knocks an opponent off his or her feet.

For Further Reading

Almeida, Bira. *Capoeira, a Brazilian Art Form: History, Philosophy, and Practice*. Berkeley, CA: North Atlantic Books, 1986.

Capoeira, Nestor. *The Little Capoeira Book*. Berkeley, CA: North Atlantic Books, 1995.

Lewis, J. Lowell, and Robert Farris Thompson. *Ring of Liberation: Deceptive Discourse in Brazilian Capoeira*. Chicago: University of Chicago Press, 1992.

Where to Learn More About Capoeira

Capoeira Angola Center of Mestre João Grande, Inc.
Mestre João Grande
69 West 14th Street, 2nd floor
New York, NY 10011
(212) 989-6975 after 5PM EST
Web site: http://www.panix.com/~
tishotto/capoeira/

Capoeira Angola Palmares
Mestre Ombrinho
c/o Afro Brazil Arts, Inc.
432 East 13th Street, #17
New York, NY 10009
(212) 677-2203
Web site:
http://home.att.net/~ombrinho/
AABA.html
e-mail: ombrinho@worldnet.att.net

Capoeira Bahia
Mestre Acordeon
2026 Addison Street
Berkeley, CA 94704
(510) 666-1255

The Capoeira Foundation at DanceBrazil
104 Franklin Street
New York, NY 10013
(212) 274-9737
Web site: http://www.capoeira-foundation.org

International Capoeira Angola Foundation
Mestre Cobra Mansa
5924 Georgia Avenue, NW
Washington, DC 20011
(800) 920-3277
Web site: http://www.capoeira-angola.org/default.asp

In Canada

Axé Capoeira Academy
Mestre Barrão
695 Smithe Street, 3rd floor
Vancouver, BC V6B 2C9
(604) 669-3135
Web site: http://mypage.direct.ca/c/camara

Web Sites

http://www.angelfire.com/tx/Capoeira/capoeira.html
http://www.blackbeltmag.com/
http://www.capoeira.com
http://www.capoeirasj.com
http://www.jangada.com/

Index

Credits

Acknowledgments

Gratitude and appreciation to the Capoeira Angola Palmares Group and its students, who appear in photographs throughout the book. Thank you for sharing your time and talent. Those pictured include Michael Goldstein (Mestre Ombrinho), Jose Cuebas, Lawrence Adams, Omitola Hill, Talia Lewis, Carmelita Cuevas, Luke Hausler, Ryan O'Donnnell, Brendan R. Lyons, John Wright, and Karl G. Peña.

Also, a special thank you to Sule Greg C. Wilson, who served as an expert reader for this project, and to Kay Torrance for further research and writing.

About the Author

Jane Atwood is a professional writer. She lives in New York City.

Photo Credits

Cover photo by John Bentham; pp. 2, 4, 8, 11, 15, 26, 28, 29, 30–31, 32, 33, 34, 36, 38, 39, 40, 41, 43, 44–45, 46, 47, 48, 49, 57 by John Bentham; p. 17 © Corbis-Bettman; p. 35 by Sean Adair; pp. 50, 52, 54 by Laura Murawski

Design and Layout

Series Design: Laura Murawski
Layout: Steve Castelli and Oliver Halsman Rosenberg

Consulting Editors

Erin M. Hovanec and Erica Smith